WILLS BEFORE 18!

Probate jurisdiction

Before 1858, the proving of wills was a matter for the ecclesiastical courts. This probably arose because the lawyer-clerics of the old church were quasi-independent of King and barons, so their dealings were more likely to be unbiased, or at least held upright by equal pressure from all directions. Even after the Establishment of the Church, the system continued, because it worked tolerably well and there was no simple alternative ready.

There were different grades of probate court:-

1. *The Archbishop's Court.* The Prerogative Court of Canterbury (PCC) dealt with the south, the Prerogative Court of York (PCY) with the north (Cheshire, Nottinghamshire and northwards). The PCC (actually in London, not Canterbury) was superior to PCY.
2. *The Bishop's Court.* The Consistory Court covered a whole diocese, the Commissary Court a designated part of it, possibly a whole county.
3. *The Archdeacon's Court.* Covered one archdeaconry only.
4. *The Peculiar or local courts.* These covered a particular parish, group of parishes or special area.

Disregarding the last category, for the moment, the normal rules for probate jurisdiction said that if a man had '*bona notabilia*' - goods worth mentioning - meaning valued at £5 or more - in one archdeaconry only, the will was proved in the Archdeacon's Court; if in two archdeaconries, then in the Commissary or Consistory Court. If he had goods in two dioceses, then in PCC or PCY. If in both provinces, then in PCC. Rules are made to be broken, and in practice executors would use the court which was convenient to them, often going to the PCC for status reasons, of for the fun of a trip to London rather than a dull provincial town. Nonconformists were particularly apt to do this, since the higher the court, the less overt connection with the church was discernable. In fact local clergy were appointed to act for the court before whom documents *could* be sworn.

Peculiars were parishes exempt from the jurisdiction of the local archdeacon, or even the bishop. They might 'report direct' to the archbishop, to some other local ecclesiastic like a dean or prebend of a cathedral, or even be under the control of the civil authority, in form of a manorial court. Wills records for peculiar courts may have fetched up miles from those of adjacent parishes.

There was a fifth place where some wills might be dealt with. Local clergy without law training but with practical experience were sometimes deputed to prove wills for the archdeacon. They were the obvious persons to deal with the estates also of those without '*bona notabilia*' in their parish, to see that the right heir got the few effects. In practice, it seems that estates which should have gone to probate officially, since they were over the limit, were also dealt with locally, by the clergyman, or by neighbours, if there was no possible dispute. There are numerous references to legacies under wills not proved in any known court.

Real and personal estate

Even allowing for the vast difference in the value of money nowadays, £5 may seem a very small sum. It must be understood that the value of a will as proved in an ecclesiastical court referred only to the personal estate, not the real estate. Real estate belonged in theory to the King, from whom his subjects held, usually through a lower lord. Therefore, the disposal of it (technically the *will*) was effected through the royal or manor courts. Personal estate came from God, so it could properly be dealt with by God's representative, the bishop. This meant that the disposal of personal estate (technically the *testament*) covered a very minor part of the testator's property, if he held land.

Real estate consisted of houses, barns, shops, mills, etc., and any sort of land and associated rights connected with it held freehold or copyhold. Land under tenancy 'by Copy of Court Roll' was held from the manor, but descended automatically from father to son, failing whom, daughters, nephew, cousins who were descended from the original grantees. It was therefore a permanent holding for practical purposes.

Personal estate consisted of household furniture and bedding, pots and pans, clothing, farm stock and equipment, tools and stock in trade, crops growing and gathered, horses, carriages, wine, food, fuel, cash in hand, debts owing, securities for money lent to others - in fact, any perishable asset. Leasehold houses and lands were included, because a lease was temporary, even a long one.

Even quite important yeomen managed with very few personal possessions. Their houses were barely furnished, their clothing limited and their need for actual cash was not great, because of the great amount of barter trading. A will made at harvest time might show large amounts of crops and cattle, whereas one made in spring would find the barns empty. The personal estate could therefore be small, and the land holding considerable. As duty was payable to the bishop on the value of the estate declared, the wise testator naturally did his best to minimise this - our ancestors may not have been able to read and write, but they knew about tax avoidance schemes. Nonconformists were particuarly adept.

Making the will

Henceforth the term 'will' is used to include both the will and testament as correctly used. Very few wills were made until the prospective testator was really aged (over 70) or in poor health. This was partly a reluctance to tempt fortune, or prospective heirs, into hastening the process; partly to retain the power of choice to the end; and partly because making a will cost effort, time and money, and no one wanted to do it twice. If a man in middle age, with a wife and family of eight, made a will, he could be reasonably sure that within a decade, his wife might die, some of his children certainly would, others might be born, he might acquire more property, or lose some, and have to rethink the sums he had given as legacies. There was also the fact that a will was a highly personal document, possibly the only chance an illiterate man had in his lifetime to express his views and opinions of his nearest and dearest. It was publicly declared, or at least to the witnesses, so a prudent man saved up his opinions until he was on his deathbed, and out of reach of retaliation.

A man who became at all ill knew that his time had come, with the primitive state of medicine then, and either wrote his will, if he knew how, or asked a friend, the parson or, later on, a lawyer, to do it for him. The practice would be for the writer to take down the provisions of the will from dictation, to go away and write it out, then come back next day and read it to the testator before witnesses. They were to attest that he was in his right mind and that he had listened to and accepted the will as correct. Then the testator and the witnesses signed or made their marks, in each others' presence. The witnesses could be, and usually were, beneficiaries under the will, who would naturally be at the deathbed.

Sometimes the process was left just too late. If the writer was slow, or the testator imminently dying, a *nuncupative* will could legally be made, in the presence of four persons. Provided the man stated what he wanted done and was sane at the time, the will could be written down afterwards and was valid though he died before signing it, as long as the witnesses agreed what he said. There is often a great deal of circumstantial detail about how he died and why there was no time to write down the will in the usual way.

What the will contains

A will normally starts with a religious preamble. Before 1700, this might read: 'In the Name of God Amen I Thomas Fludde of Little Notley in the county of X beinge sicke and weake in bodye but thanks be to God of goode and perfect rememberance do constitute and make this my last will and testament in manner and forme followinge that is to say first I bequeathe my sowle unto Almightye God my saviour and redeemer and my body to the earth from whence it came to be buryed at the discresion of mine executor hereinafter named and touchinge those worldly goods with which it hath pleased God to bless me...'.

This does not mean that the ancestor was particularly religious. The court was ecclesiastical, so the phrases were too. There might be an element of hedging bets by a man on his death-bed, but the grudging bequest of a few pence for 'tithes forgot' and sums for the upkeep of the bells and the altar, in early wills, often covers a lifetime of battling with the Church over those tithes. The fulsome religious phrases were mostly toned down in the secular eighteenth century, but are sometimes found in total as later as 1820.

Charitable bequests sometimes come next, varying from a few shillings to the local poor on the day of the funeral (sometimes distributed as beer and bread to the poor who carried the coffin) to regular doles on the anniversary of the death (the 'year's minde') or in perpetuity. If the last, there should be local records of administration as a charity. The direction to bury the body matters, if it is in the church, rather than churchyard (shows wealth or standing) or in a parish other than that of residence (?place of origin).

The next provision is usually that for the wife, which varies according to income, but is basically for house-room and income. If she is referred to as 'my now wife', there have been others. Conventional provision would be a small house or specified rooms in the family home, or just 'room and board' with the eldest son for life. If she is a step-mother, the terms of the legacy are likely to be very clearly set out, with precise rooms, rights, goods and services to which she is entitled. A widow is likely to be left an annuity, chargeable on the profits arising from the family business, or from the various family properties, often shared between a number of sons, each paying a small sum to her quarterly.

Sometimes, this financial legacy, possibly with a lump sum added, is said to be 'in lieu of her thirds' (or of widows' bench or dower). Strictly, a widow was entitled to a third of the real estate for life, which could be inconvenient if an adult son wished to run a farm or business as a unit. If the children were small, a widow might be left the main estate until they were adult, or even for life. A more usual provision is to limit this by adding 'if she remain my widow'. If she married again, she would lose house-room and all or most of her legacy. This was partly male chauvinist piggery, but partly an attempt to safeguard the interests of the children, for a new husband would take possession of all that she owned on marriage. A widow might be left household goods, or a share of them for life only or 'absolutely' or 'at her own dispose', which meant that she could sell or bequeath them in her turn. A wealthy man might even leave her a house and land for herself.

If no provision at all is made in the will for house-room for the widow, this has almost certainly been otherwise catered for by a marriage settlement earlier. A widow could not simply be thrown out when her husband died, even where relations were not good. She would have legal redress, which would be expensive, but would impoverish the family estate as well, so few men would risk it.

Next comes the provision for the children. Normally, the eldest son would inherit the major part of the real estate. In the case of copyhold, this was automatic, and no mention would necessarily be made in the will. Most freeholds were likely to be 'limited' when purchased, to the man and his 'heirs', which meant first the eldest son. If these conditions are met, then the will may appear to leave nothing to this son, but to charge him with the payment of money legacies to his younger brothers and sisters. If the son is appointed executor, it is probable that he does inherit the main real estate even if this is not stated.

Younger sons may be given a secondary real estate, if this is available, in which case it must be stated. Otherwise, they are generally given a sum to apprentice them, or to set them up in business. The payment may be at 21, the standard age for receiving legacies, or postponed for some years, so that a heavy demand for cash does not cripple the family estate.

Daughters are generally given a money dowry, at 21 or a prior marriage with the consent of their guardian. Only if the father has a great deal of land is he likely to give this to a daughter. An eldest daughter occasionally gets more than the others. Daughters unmarried at their father's death were expected to live with their mother, or eldest brother, till they married. Sometimes a father would provide a cottage or annuity for a middle-aged daughter expected to remain a spinster.

Because a husband took his wife's property, a father who was suspicious of his son-in-law might leave a legacy to someone else on behalf of his daughter, to be advanced 'at his discretion as best he can arrange' and only paid to the girl if she became a widow. She might be given a life interest only, with remainder to her children after her death. Sometimes this was done to give the family an income they could rely on, if the husband was in debt, for sums paid wholly to her would be seized by his creditors.

Occasionally, a wealthy man may leave certain of his children twelve pence (or other token sum) only. This is often referred to as '*cutting off with a shilling*' and regarded as proof of ill feeling. However, it often means that the adult son or daughter has already had his portion or her dowry from the estate. It is usually totally clear when the testator dislikes one of his children, because he says so. 'To my son John, twelve pence of current money, if he come and demand it, since he has been ungrateful and ill conditioned to his mother and myself these many years.'

Because these wills were made for illiterates and hand copied by clerks, it was wise to include the names of all the children, even if they were to be 'cut off', since otherwise it was open for the aggrieved son to claim that his name had been omitted in the copying. The remark above makes Father's feelings quite clear.

If a man died leaving young children, or left a legacy to infant grandchildren, he would, if he were prudent, allow for at least some of them to die before the legacy was paid, usually at the legal age of majority, 21, or at such other age as the testator appointed. A daughter, in particular, might marry under age and die leaving issue, in which case he could allow the child or children to inherit what the mother would have received. He could order that the share of a child who died should go to the survivors of that group (benefit of survivorship), to another person, or back to the estate. If it reverted to the estate, it formed part of the *residue*.

Real estate would normally go to 'the eldest son and his heirs (or heirs male) forever', but a father determined to keep it in the family might *entail* it, by leaving it to the heirs *of the body* of the eldest son, then the second son, and his heirs of the body, and so on. It was often limited to the heirs male of the body of each son in turn, then to the eldest son of a named brother and his heirs male and so on (tail male). Only if the male heirs failed were the females let in, as heirs general, or right heirs. This is the way peerages descend mostly. If you find an entailed property in the family from way back, to which you appear to be entitled, forget it. Entails were broken in the nineteenth century and property cannot be left to generations far distant in the future. The only limitation which can be made is to living persons and those born within 21 years of the testator's death. 'Perpetuities' for land or money therefore failed.

However, attempts to establish an entail can lead to a very fine list of family names, all given with their relationships, often expressed as 'my nephew John son of my late brother William' and so on. The process whereby X will inherit if Y dies childless is called a *remainder* and can be written down briefly as 'If X dsp rem. to Y' or, for male descent, 'If X dspm, rem. to Y'.

If the will refers to 'surrendering (land) to the uses of my will' it means that the property is copyhold, held from some manor, often named. An estate left to persons as *joint tenants* is owned by them, not as tenants in the modern sense, and the survivor takes all. If they hold as *tenants in common*, they are also owners and their heirs will inherit the individual shares.

Married women could not make a will leaving property, even if they were heiresses. On marriage, their husband took the lot and could do as he wished with it - even the clothes in which they stood up could be given away. Even if real estate was left to her and her children after her death, the husband could claim a life interest, which was difficult to prevent. He would be owner as guardian of children under

21 anyway. Towards the end of the period, some advanced fathers left property to their daughters which they specified she could bequeath 'by will or deed in writing'. This deed needed the cooperation of the husband, could only deal with the property or money named, and it was a tough lady who dared to leave it other than to her husband or their children.

Widows and maiden aunts could and did make wills, and very often these are excellent value from the genealogical point of view, leaving small legacies and trinkets to every member of a large clan by name and description. If no will is to be found for a lady who obviously lived in affluent circumstances, it may be that she had a life interest only in all she possessed, which was then remaindered to another member of the family, under the will of husband or father.

Many wills contained bequests of 'mourning rings' to a large number of relatives and friends. Portrait lockets were also popular and, at the end of the period, brooches or lockets containing the hair of the deceased or a dead child. Silver spoons were passed down the family from generation to generation, and might be engraved with family initials. In many wills, the testator's clothing was divided among family and servants. A richly embroidered gown was a valuable gift and even everyday wear had a lot of use in it still, so these were legacies worth having. It is possible to sketch a pciture of what a person wore from some wills.

The will should finish with a bequest of the residue of the estate, expressed as 'all other my goods and chattels, moveable and immoveable'. This covers everything not specifically bequeathed, including assets acquired after the will was made, if there is time. If no bequest of residue was made, then this should technically have been treated as if the person died intestate. In practice, the executor would probably take it. If a legatee died before the testator, or before getting the legacy, then this money would also fall into the residue if not otherwise directed. This rarely happened, since testators normally did a remainder.

An *executor* or executors were appointed - an *executrix* if female - who had to arrange the burial in a manner fitting the station of the deceased, pay and collect debts, prove the will - often done within a matter of days of the death - and arrange for the making of an inventory of the deceased's estate (see over). Only after the full extent of the estate was established could he decide how much some of the legacies were worth. The will often directed that certain sums - for mourning or for the living expenses of the widow - should be paid immediately on death. Other legacies might be delayed for six or twelve months, to enable cash to be raised on an estate consisting of land or goods.

Legacies to minors were not due until the recipient was 21 or married, or some other age if the testator directed. Other bequests were postponed until after the death of the widow or another person with a life rent. Therefore the involvement of the executor with the estate might go on for years, and he would have to keep track of

In the Name of God Amen I William Leech of Wootton in the County of Oxon Labourer being in health of Body and of Sound and disposing Mind and Understanding praised be God do make this my last Will and Testament in manner following and first I will that all my just debts and Funerall Expences be paid and discharged. Item. I give and devise All That my Messuage or Tenement with the Garden and all and singular other the premises thereunto belonging situate and being in Wootton aforesaid wherein I now dwell (after my wifes decease) unto my daughter Sarah and her heirs for ever. Item I give unto my Son Thomas One Shilling. Item I give the use of all my houshold goods unto my loving wife for the Terme of her life and after her decease I give the said houshold goods unto my said daughter. Item I give all the rest of my Estate unto my loving wife Elizabeth and her Assignes and do hereby make my said wife my sole Executrix. In Witness whereof I have hereunto set my hand and Seale the Ninth day of June in the Fourth Year of the Reigne of King George the Second and in the Year of Our Lord 1731

Signed Sealed Published and Declared by the said William Leech the Testator as and for his last Will and Testament in the Presence of us and then Subscribed by us as Witnesses at his request and in his presence

William Leech
his mark

Thos: Ryves
Mary Fowler
John [illegible]

births and deaths in the family and recalculate the entitlement of all recipients. In most cases, a member of the family was chosen to act. The widow was often executrix for life or while she remained unmarried, with the eldest son or a brother. A minor could be appointed as executor, though he could not act until he was 21 - by which time there would be plenty of work to do. The will would be proved by the living adult executor, with 'power reserved' for the minor (or for any other executor who did not turn up on the same day. If a minor was the sole surviving executor named, then a guardian, normally the next of kin, acted for him till he was of age. The executor could witness the will and benefit from it and was normmaly given something for his trouble, which might be great.

Overseers - normally two or three - were appointed until at least 1750 to ensure that the executor carried out the provisions of the will properly. They were usually mature relatives - brothers, cousins, uncles - or respected friends, though sometimes the parson or the local resident gentleman was chosen. They were expected to advise a widow and children and to take action in any dispute between the legatees (over division of furniture, for example) or between legatees and the executor. The Big Brother function was vaguely defined and how long it continued depended on the age and interest of the individual.

When the will was first proved, the executor/s had to estimate the value of the estate and take out a *bond* for twice that amount that they would administer faithfully and that they would produce an inventory of the deceased's property, in a set time, normally a year. This *inventory*, covering the personal estate only, was to be made by 'two indifferent men' - which means two unbiased persons - normally two neighbours of the same status as the deceased, who could estimate very exactly what his goods and crops were worth. They went round

Left: A typical eighteenth century will, that made by William Leech of Wootton, Oxon., in 1731. That he was a labourer shows that all classes may leave wills. Note his wife's life interest in the family home and the token shilling legacy to his son. The will was proved (below) five years later in the Court of the Archdeacon of Oxford (reproduced by permission of the Oxfordshire County Record Office, ref. MS Wills Oxon 140/1/15).

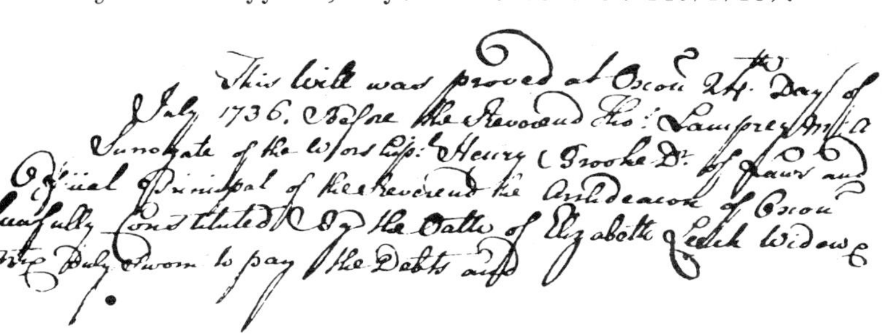
This will was proved at Oxon 24th Day of July 1736. Before the Reverend Tho: Lamprey Mr Surrogate of the Worshipful Henry Brooke Dr of Laws and Official Principal of the Reverend the Archdeacon of Oxon lawfully Constituted By the Oath of Elizabeth Leech Widow Executrix Duly Sworn to pay the Debts and

his house, listing the contents of each room, usually in detail, then round the farm yard and fields, or the shop, then they added details of debts owed and owing, bonds for loans or mortgages, and any leasehold property. These inventories were returned to the court and are often filed with the wills, or in a separate series. They were at their most detailed in the Elizabethan and pre-Civil War period. Later ones often only give the total value of 'the goods in the house' or some such phrase. Where they survive - and many have been lost or wantonly destroyed - they give a fascinating picture of the way of life of our ancestors and the exact furnishing of their houses. They are mostly found in local courts, with very varying rates of survival; those for PCC only survive from 1661 to the early years of the eighteenth century (see page 15).

Intestacy. Where a person died without making a will at all, but with goods to the value of £5 or more, *administration* of the estate was granted to the next of kin, provided that he or she was over 21. A married woman could be administratrix, though she would have had trouble stopping her husband from meddling. If minor children only were left, a guardian - usually the adult male next of kin - was appointed to act. A widow - called the *relict* or left over - was next of kin of a deceased man, and took a third of all his estate, for life, though she might be entitled to more under a marriage settlement.

In some manors, she got less than a third of a copyhold, unless the husband had arranged a life interest for her. After 1833, 'widow's thirds' were barred, and the whole estate went to the heir at law. This could be her eldest son, a step-son or a nephew or more distant relation of her husband. Entailed estates, in which the husband had only a life interest, went directly to the heir of the remainder anyway, so she could lose husband and home at once.

Personal estate was shared between the wife and children - and this was all the younger children of a family got under primogeniture. If there were no children, then shares went to the parents, brothers and sisters, grandparents, uncles and aunts, in that order, with preference to the nearest class of relative and to males over females. If there were no close relatives, the Crown took everything except copyholds, which reverted to the lord of the manor.

Encumbered estates. Debts and various charges might reduce the apparent value of an estate. Money was often due under marriage settlements, to the widow (or father's widow), for annuities to younger children and other relatives or for mortgages (which were payable out of personal estate, often reducing still further the amount the widow and younger children got). In extreme circumstances, debts might outweigh assets, and then a major creditor might be appointed to administer the estate, paying himself first, and the rest as best he might. Only the cost of the funeral and legal fees for proving the will took precedence of debts. The widow was entitled to her 'paraphernalia', meaning her clothing and very basic personal effects - rarely including jewellery or anything of value, even if it had been hers before marriage.

Alternative methods of property transfer

If no will is found in any court for an apparently wealthy person, it is possible that the estate passed by entail, or under an ancestor's will. A widow was often left a life interest only, which died with her, and even her clothes might not be 'at her own dispose'.

Most families from yeoman farmers upwards drew up some form of *marriage settlement*, whereby the bride's father gave money (or land) and the intending groom promised to settle on her specific property, to the value of the dowry at least. If there were children, it would pass to them on the death of both parents. If the girl died childless, the property reverted to whoever had provided most money. The property of a major heiress would belong to her husband while he lived, but a prudent father would tie it up so that he could not sell it, or bequeath it elsewhere.

Deeds of gift were another common device, often used by nonconformists. A father could make over part of his estate to a son on marriage, sometimes for an annual payment. Household goods were commonly given in this way. An elderly person often made over his whole estate in return for accommodation and maintenance in a married child's household for life. Occasionally these deeds are proved like a will - mostly if some other member of the family objected, but usually they are kept in family archives or among lawyers' papers.

Even copyholds could be 'sold' for a nominal figure to a member of the family who was not heir at law. If it was done without agreement by the heir, there may be a dispute, but otherwise, the only record is in the manorial rolls. A son leaving to take up a trade in the town might have no interest in a small agricultural holding, and as long as he got a money portion, he was content (St. Luke, XV, 11-13,31).

Apart from these relatively formal methods, it is apparent that a great deal of property must have passed by informal gifts during life or on the death bed, or was quietly removed by those who had charge of the dying person, especially if the heir was absent. Many families tried to by-pass the expense of the probate court in cases where there was a simple family set-up, and for every one who was caught, dozens must have escaped. This accounts for a lot of 'missing wills'.

Where to locate wills

At the change to civil courts in 1858, probate records from many of the old ecclesiastical registries were centralised at Somerset House. In the 1950s/60s this process was reversed, and the records from the local courts were all redistributed to the appropriate diocesan record offices. In England these are normally the county record offices, with the following major exceptions:

Cambridgeshire: Cambridge University Library;
Derbyshire, Staffordshire, part of Shropshire: Lichfield J.R.O.;
Durham and Northumberland: University of Durham;
Rutland: Northamptonshire Record Office;
Surrey: Greater London Record Office;
Yorkshire: mainly at the Borthwick Institute, York.

Records for *London and Middlesex* are mainly split between Guildhall Library and the G.L.R.O.; some for *Shropshire* are at Hereford or the National Library of Wales; for *Warwickshire* are split between Lichfield and Worcester; and for *Westmorland* are split between Cumbria R.O., Carlisle and Lancashire R.O., Preston. Those for *Wales and Monmouthshire* are at the National Library of Wales, Aberystwyth.

There are, however, plenty of anomalies, where dioceses have not been coterminous with counties and where peculiars have included parishes in more than one county. The key to the various courts, their geographical coverage, and the present location, extent of and indexes to their records is J.S.W. Gibson's *A Simplified Guide to Probate Jurisdictions: Where to Look for Wills*, now in its third edition (1985), published by the FFHS at £2.00. There are also two earlier and more substantial books, published in 1974, and thus now rather out-of-date, but found in many libraries and bibliographies. These are Gibson's *Wills and Where to Find Them*, which is the easier for the beginner to follow, and the fourth edition of *Wills and their Whereabouts*, by A.J. Camp. This latter is the most authoritative book on the subject, with much detail of the different types of probate records surviving for different courts. For the more experienced this can be very useful, but for those just starting it can be rather intimidating and confusing, as it is arranged by courts rather than the places to which they refer.

In these books lists of the parishes which belonged to peculiar jurisdictions or outlying parts of dioceses are given. Full addresses and locations of the various repositories can be found in *Record Offices: How to Find Them*, by Jeremy Gibson and Pamela Peskett, FFHS, third edition, 1985, £1.00.

Many indexes to these wills, and other records, have been printed and many more card-indexed in the repository concerned. Those without modern indexes should have semi-contemporary manuscript indexes, some made annually, some for blocks of years. They may be calendars - that is, a list of wills grouped by the first letter of the surname, not in absolute alphabetical order.

Copying wills and abstracting information

If you know the precise date of death of an ancestor, you can either use the index personally, or ask the record office concerned to check and send a photocopy of the will to you. They will normally do this if given exact information, but cannot undertake long searches in the indexes - especially in calendars - for someone undated, or for 'everyone called Bloggs'. They also cannot take time to make an abstract of the will for you, but may be able to recommend a searcher. Make sure that the searcher can really cope with the old writing and understands what the will means - there are far too many inexpert people in the trade now. Unless you know a reliable person, send for a photostat and transcribe at your leisure.

If at all possible, make an *abstract* of the will yourself. An example of reducing a page to a few lines is given in my *Somerset House Wills* (and advice on reading the writing in *Old Handwriting* in this series, obtainable from the author only at present).

Basically, you should note:

- The name of the testator;
- The place where he lived and his occupation if stated;
- Special directions for burial;
- The names of all legatees and the full details of the legacies;
- Whether they were given for life only, for widowhood only, at a specified age;
- What happens to the legacy if the first named person died;
- Any odd clauses or personal comments on relatives;
- The precise date when the will was made, and the probate date;
- The names of executor(s), overseers and witnesses.

Although the dates are usually very close together, a sick person might recover, an old person last longer than expected. Legatees and executors may have died in the intervening period. The probate declaration immediately follows the will in the register copy, or is written on the back of an original will. If only one named executor proved the will, note if he is called 'surviving executor' or if 'power is reserved' to the other/s. Before the eighteenth century, this declaration will probably be in Latin. It should still be easy to pick out the name of the person proving the will, with some such descriptive word(s) as 'relict' (the widow) or 'filius' (son) amongst the legal verbiage - the other name will be that of the judge or court official before whom it was proved.

Inventories may be with the wills, or separately kept in the same office, or missing. Always ask. Administrations (*admons.*) may also be separated. They give limited information - normally only the name of the next of kin and his/her relationship to the deceased, unless guardians have to be appointed for minors. There are occasionally other documents connected with probate, some of which, accounts for instance, can be quite informative. Definitions of these are given in the Glossary in *A Simplified Guide to Probate Jurisdictions*.

PCC Wills

The richer folk, who might have property in more than one diocese, tended to have wills proved in the Prerogative Court of Canterbury. So did those who wished to be thought the family had, or those whose executors fancied a trip to London (though business could be done locally too), or were nonconformists who sought to avoid the local church dignitaries. Use of this 'top' court was far more widespread throughout the social spectrum than is generally realised, and a search for wills should always include PCC. For instance, towards the end of the period, the Bank of England would only accept probate from PCC. These wills are now kept at the Public Record Office in London, at Chancery Lane.

Wills of soldiers and sailors, of those with property abroad, or who died in 'parts beyond the seas', also had to be proved in PCC. From 1654 to 1660, the bishops were no longer allowed to act as probate officials, and all wills had officially to be proved in London, at a civil registry, though many possessors of small estates managed to avoid this by making alternative arrangements or not bothering to prove unless someone informed on them.

Anyone may consult the PCC wills, after getting a Reader's Ticket for the P.R.O. from the office in the gatehouse at Chancery Lane. It is a rapid process for adult British subjects who can produce evidence of identity. The wills are kept upstairs (enquire on first visit) and you will need to use pencils in the search room.

Alphabetical indexes (available in good large reference libraries) have been printed for blocks of years from the earliest (1383) up to 1700. These indexes include the parish of residence of the testator. These, at least for most of the seventeenth century and earlier, use a system of reference which has since been modified, but is still adequate to lead you easily enough to the will when you are actually at the P.R.O. They will also be accepted if you are ordering a photocopy by post. This old system had been to allot to each year a 'name', usually that of a prominent testator. Thus the indexes for the early period will give as reference, a name and number, rather than an actual year date (and remember that the year it represents is that of probate, not necessarily the same as death). The number will be the 'quire' number, see right. At the P.R.O. you will find the 'name' has been dispensed with and the annual calendars are identified by date.

From 1700 to 1749, the only source of reference is the manuscript calendars at the P.R.O. itself - these are annual lists of wills by the first letter of the surname only, followed by admons. in similar lists, in order of the date when the will was proved or the administration was taken out. Only the county of probate is given, or 'Pts' (ie Foreign Parts) for those living or dying abroad. This makes it quite difficult to trace a person with a common name who died in London. There may be several 'John Brown, Middx.' entries in a year.

From 1750 to 1800 the Society of Genealogists (14 Charterhouse Buildings, Goswell Road, London EC1M 7BA) has a composite card index, fully alphabetical, to all wills (not admons.) in PCC. This only gives the information provided by the calendars, ie year, month and county of probate, and the quire number. The index is in process of publication, three volumes covering A to G being available. A search of the remainder can be undertaken by staff at the Society for a fee, but the index is not open to use by members or the public.

From 1801 to 1852 the main reference is again the annual calendars, but from 1796 on there is an alternative in the Death Duty Registers (also at the P.R.O.), which from 1812 on also index the 'Country Courts', thus providing a partial consolidated index for the whole country. Their use is far from simple, and is explained in *The Records of the PCC and the Death Duty Registers*, by Jane Cox, P.R.O., 1980.

For the last few years, 1853 to January 1858, there is a printed index, available in a few record offices and libraries (locations given in *A Simplified Guide to Probate Jurisdictions*).

To locate a PCC will at the P.R.O., you first find the reference number in the calendar for that year. There is a simple key index on the counter (which will if necessary 'translate' the 'name' you may have from a published index into the year). Against the year, pick out the group of numbers within which your own reference number occurs. The number which is level with this group is the piece number you need to order. It will probably (for the older wills) be presented to you on a microfilm, white on black (rather nasty for reading, but you get used to it quickly enough), or as a very hefty register book. When you have the film or book, first find the quire number. This is not a page, but a gathering of sixteen pages. Look for a large handwritten figure in the the right hand corner of every sixteenth page, and ignore the smaller, machine-stamped, figure which occurs on every page. When you have your quire number, start looking for the will, which could be anywhere in the next sixteen pages. If you come to the next quire number, back track. When you've found your will, it's worth noting the alternative (page) number, for your own future reference.

With the old references from the published indexes you can order a photocopy by post (or when you are at the P.R.O.). The staff will locate it within its sixteen pages. The cost per sheet (at September 1985) is 80p per sheet if it can be taken from a microfilmed register, or £2.00 per sheet if it has to be taken from a volume or original will that has not been filmed. As PCC wills are often very long, this can be expensive; and it is sure to take some time.

Inventories for PCC testators only survive from 1661 to the early years of the eighteenth century. There are modern indexes, partly published (see 'Inventories in the records of PCC', by J.S.W. Gibson, *The Local Historian*, **14**, 4, November 1980).

PCY wills

For northerners, the equivalent of PCC was the Prerogative Court of York (PCY), whose records are at the Borthwick Institute in York. The counties covered were Cheshire, Cumberland, Durham, the southern detachment of Flintshire, Lancashire, Northumberland, Nottinghamshire, Westmorland and Yorkshire (also the Isle of Man). Indexes have been published to 1688, a modern consolidated index for 1688-1731 exists, with calendars as for PCC for the remainder of the period (both on microfilm at the Society of Genealogists).

Devon and Somerset

Wills for these counties were mostly destroyed at Exeter during the War. Copies from the Estate Duty Office have been handed over to the respective county record offices, but they are incomplete and mostly date only from 1800. Many abstracts of Devon wills were made by Miss Moger before the loss, and some wills of Somerset gentry and connected families by Crisp. A great effort has recently been made by the record offices in both counties to collect copies of wills in private hands, from manorial records or quoted in land transfers.

Scotland

Probate was taken out of the Church's hands in 1560, but the new Commissariot Courts covered diocesan areas. Edinburgh was the over-riding court. All wills before 1823 are at the Scottish Record Office, General Register House, Edinburgh EH1 3YY. Most wills after 1823 are too, but others are at various sheriff courts (see *A Simplified Guide to Probate Jurisdictions*). Indexes to all courts to 1800 have been published by the Scottish Record Society.

Ireland

Here the vast majority of wills were destroyed with other Irish records in 1922, but determined efforts have been made to collect every remaining copy in private hands. The Public Record Offices in Dublin (Four Courts, Dublin) and Belfast (Balmoral Avenue, Belfast, N.I.) have printed lists of what they hold, including numerous abstracts made by genealogists in the past. The Belfast Office also has Estate Duty Office copies of wills from 1821 to 1857. Irish residents (and Scottish, for that matter) with any property in England had their wills 'resealed' in London, and copies will be found among PCC wills.

Abstracts made by the antiquary, Sir William Betham, from wills proved in the Prerogative Court of Armagh (PCC equivalent) are fairly complete and are at P.R.O. Dublin (microfilm copy at the Society of Genealogists). Other large collections of abstracts are held by the Church of Ireland Library (Church House, Church Avenue, Rathmines, Dublin 6), both Record Offices and the Society of Friends (6 Eustace Street, Dublin).